Angel Island

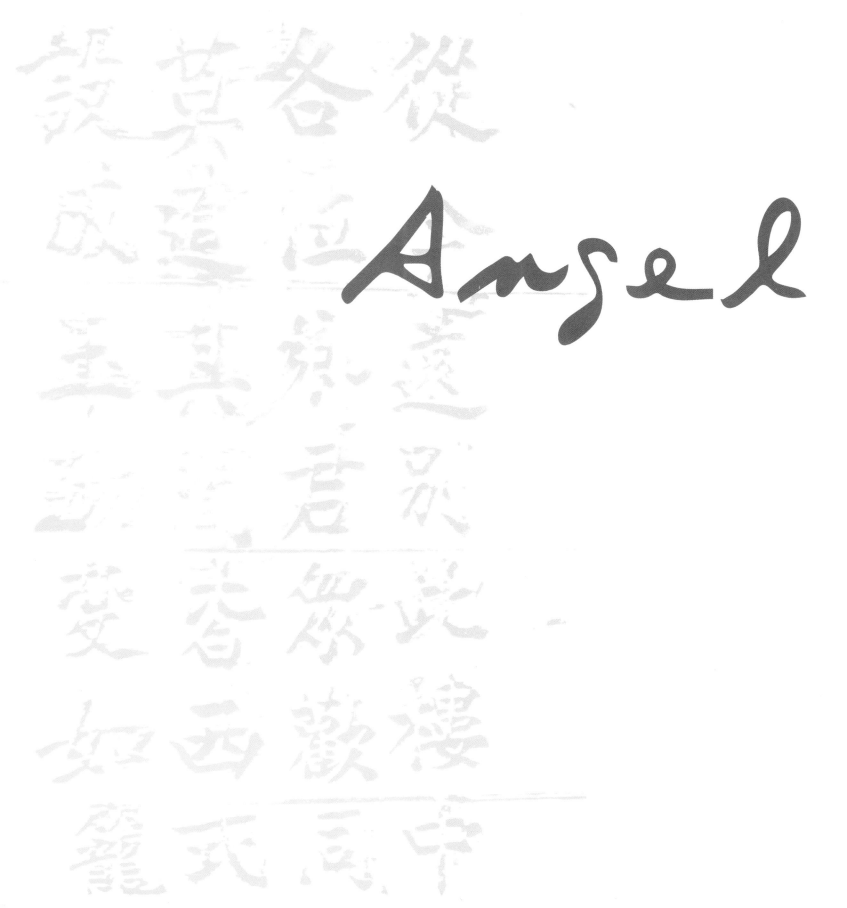

Island

GATEWAY TO GOLD MOUNTAIN

Russell Freedman

Chinese Poems Translated by Evans Chan

CLARION BOOKS

Houghton Mifflin Harcourt

Boston • New York

Endpapers: wall carvings in the detention barracks.

Clarion Books
215 Park Avenue South
New York, New York 10003

Clarion Books is an imprint of Houghton Mifflin Harcourt Publishing Company.
www.hmhbooks.com

The text was set in Berling.
Book design by Trish Parcell Watts

Library of Congress Cataloging-in-Publication Data
Freedman, Russell.
Angel Island : gateway to Gold Mountain / Russell Freedman ; Chinese poems translated by Evans Chan.
p. cm.
Includes bibliographical references.
ISBN 978-0-547-90378-1 (hardcover)
1. Angel Island (Calif.)—History—Juvenile literature. 2. Angel Island Immigration Station (Calif.)—History—
Juvenile literature. 3. San Francisco Bay Area (Calif.)—Emigration and immigration—History—Juvenile
literature. 4. United States—Emigration and immigration—History—Juvenile literature. 5. Asia—Emigration and
immigration—History—Juvenile literature. I. Title.
F868.S156F74 2013
979.4'6—dc23
2012036532

Manufactured in China
SCP 10 9 8 7 6 5 4 3 2
4500459321

To Ivan Chi-lap Ng
who found a new home in North America

Contents

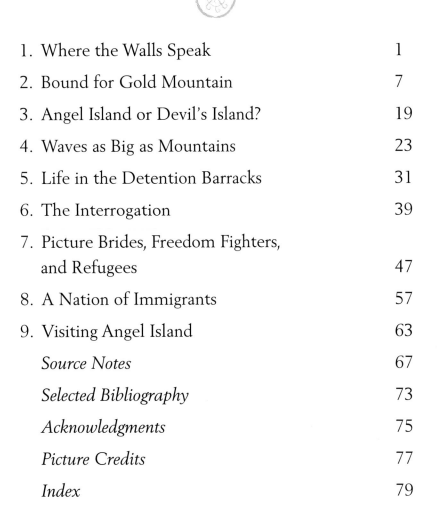

Angel Island: The Ellis Island of the West. The cover of a book published in 1917.

Where the Walls Speak

Alexander Weiss had just started his job as a California state park ranger on Angel Island in San Francisco Bay when he came across an old abandoned building. Off-limits to the public, its windows boarded up, the two-story wooden structure stood dark and deserted behind a barbed-wire fence. On an impulse, Weiss decided to venture inside and look around.

He pulled open the door. The floor creaked as he entered. The electricity had long since been turned off, so he found his way through the empty rooms and up the stairs with his flashlight, stepping over litter and broken glass. Paint was peeling from the walls and ceiling. The building smelled musty.

In a large room on the second floor, Weiss noticed markings that seemed to be carved into the walls. Moving closer, he saw that the marks appeared to be Chinese calligraphy, covered by a thin layer of chipped paint.

"I looked around and shined my flashlight up and I could see that the entire walls were covered with calligraphy, and that was what blew me away," he remembered. "People had carved the stuff on every square inch of wall space, not just in this one room but all over."

Although he couldn't read the inscriptions, he recognized their historical importance. Angel Island had once been a busy immigration station, where people hoping to enter the United States were examined and questioned and often held for days or weeks or even months while immigration officials decided their fate. For many immigrants, Angel Island was the gateway to a new life in America. But for others—those who were denied entry to the United States—it was a locked gate through which they caught just a glimpse of America before they were sent back to their native land.

While waiting for their cases to be decided, Chinese immigrants

The arrivals pier at the Angel Island Immigration Station, 1915.

carved or painted row after row of poems on the walls of their detention barracks, telling of their long voyages from China, their confinement on the lonely island, their longing for families back home, their hopes, frustration, anger, and despair. And while Chinese were the most numerous immigrants to pass through Angel Island, immigrants from all over the world left wall inscriptions of various kinds in Japanese, Korean, Russian, Punjabi, Spanish, Italian, German, and English.

When Weiss reported his discovery, he was told that the calligraphy and other inscriptions were just "a bunch of graffiti" and to forget about them. The abandoned building was about to be torn down, part of the island's redevelopment as a state park.

But Weiss couldn't forget. He felt so strongly about the historical importance of his discovery, he was willing to risk his job to help save the poems and inscriptions on the detention barracks

IMMIGRATION STATION,
ANGEL ISLAND CAL.
COPYRIGHT 1915

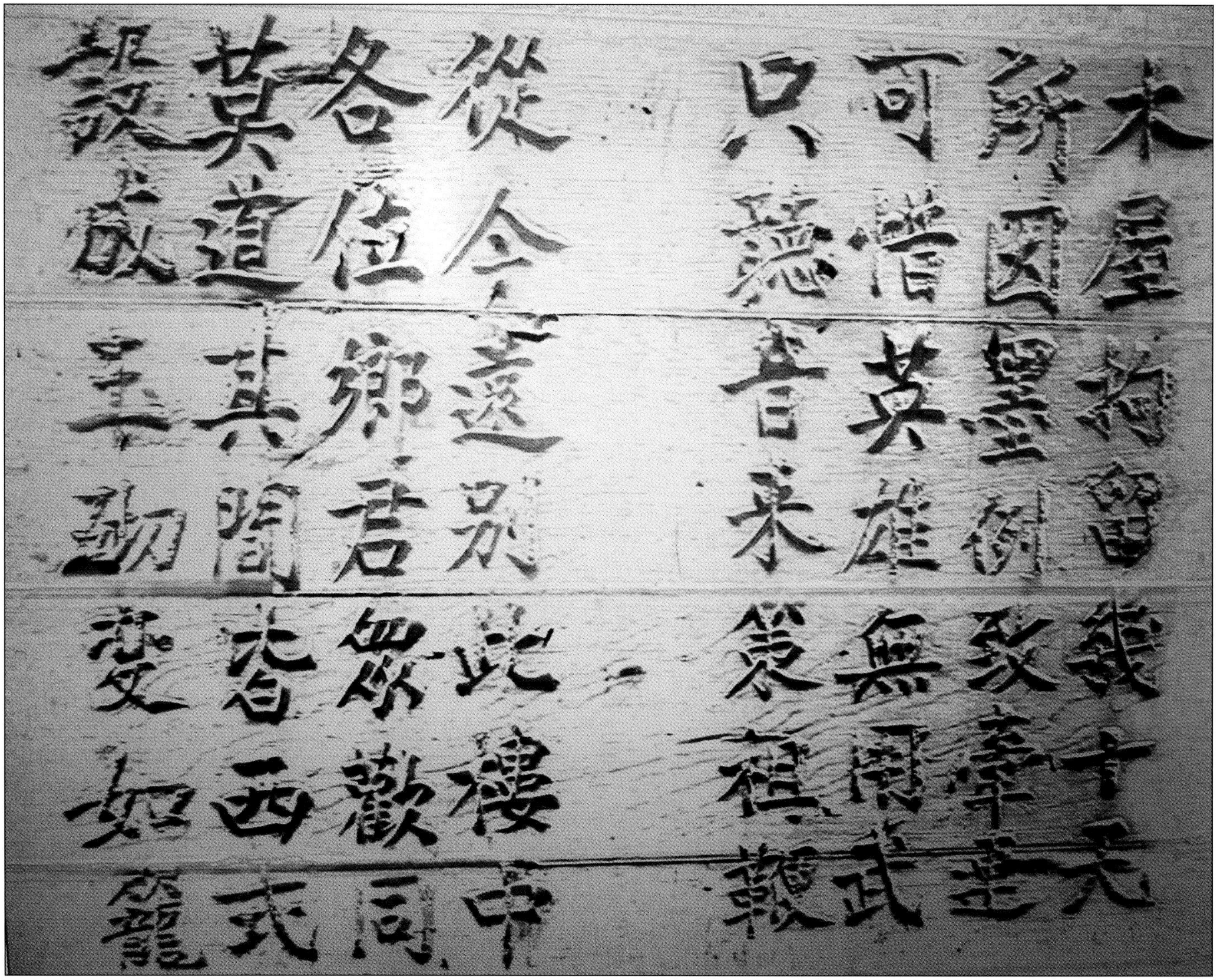

木屋拘留幾十天

辭國圖謀致審查

可惜英雄無用武

只為家貧來異邦

從今遠別此樓中

各位鄉君多珍重

莫道其間皆西式

報效...

Two Chinese poems carved into a wall in the detention barracks.

walls. "Actually, I am also an immigrant," he explained, "so I have an empathy with immigrants."

Born in Vienna, Austria, Weiss had been brought to America as a four-year-old Jewish refugee when his parents fled from the Holocaust during World War II. "I didn't discover the poems," he insisted. "They had been there for years, and other people knew they were there. But I am proud of the fact that I was able to [help save them]."

He came across the poems on an afternoon in May 1970. When his superior told him not to bother with them, Weiss alerted George Araki, who had been his biology professor at San Francisco State College. The professor's mother had come through Angel Island as a Japanese immigrant. Araki went to the island to see the poems for himself, and he had a photographer take pictures of every inch of wall that had inscriptions.

After Araki showed the photos at a meeting of the Asian American Studies Department, students and faculty began to ride the ferry out to Angel Island to view the wall poems. "They were all young Asian American students," Weiss recalled, "whose parents and grandparents had come through Angel Island, but they had no idea of this history because their parents would not talk about it."

As word spread, activists in the Asian American community launched a campaign to save the Angel Island Immigration Station. "I really felt it in my bones that this was a story that needed to be told," said journalist Chris Chow, "a historic landmark that needed to be saved."

A Chinese miner pans for gold along a California river during the 1850s.

Bound for Gold Mountain

When news of the California gold rush reached China in 1848, thousands of able-bodied young men left their ancestral homes and set out for *Gam Saan*, or Gold Mountain, as California was known. The gold seekers came mostly from poor fishing and rice-growing villages in the Pearl River delta, where poverty and famine, floods, drought, wars, and rebellion had long prompted the most enterprising men to seek their fortune in distant lands.

"There were four in our family, my mother, my father, my sister, and me," one immigrant recalled. "We lived in a two room house. Our sleeping room and the other served as parlor, kitchen and dining room. We were not rich enough to keep pigs or fowl, otherwise, our small house would have been more than overcrowded. . . .

"Sometimes we went hungry for days. My mother and me would go over the harvested rice fields of the peasants to pick the grains they dropped. . . . We had only salt and water to eat with the rice."

Many of the gold seekers were married. Hoping to strike it rich, they bid their families farewell and begged or borrowed enough money to make their way to Hong Kong, where they booked passage on ships bound for San Francisco.

"Our baggage consisted of a roll of bedding and a bamboo basket," said one early immigrant. "Into this we put our shoes, hat, and all our worldly possessions."

By 1853, some 25,000 Chinese immigrants had reached the gold fields. They called themselves Guests of Gold Mountain, but they found that many Americans did not welcome them. Violence flared as gangs of white miners crying "California for Americans!" drove the Chinese from the most productive gold fields, forcing them to work "washed-out" claims long since abandoned by the Americans.

A special tax, the Foreign Miners' Tax, was aimed mainly at the Chinese. They became the target of discriminatory laws, restricting where they could live and work. Like other nonwhites in California at the time, Chinese were not allowed to vote, marry whites, or testify in court. And unlike immigrants from Europe, they could not apply to become naturalized citizens.

A few successful Chinese miners packed up their riches and returned home, where the women they married became known as Gold Mountain Wives. But as the gold ran out, most Chinese in California abandoned their dreams of wealth. Locked out of many occupations, they took low-paying factory jobs; worked as farm laborers or domestic servants; or opened laundries, restaurants, and shops. The first Chinese laundry in San Francisco, established in 1851, was followed by a thousand more.

During the 1860s, a new wave of Chinese immigrants helped build the Central Pacific Railroad, the western leg of the first transcontinental railroad. They were hired by Charles Crocker, a railroad magnate who figured that if the Chinese could build the Great Wall, they could certainly lay tracks over the rugged

Chinese laborers on a railroad handcar. By 1867, 12,000 Chinese were employed by the Central Pacific Railroad, representing 90 percent of the entire workforce.

A Central Pacific train emerges from a snowshed in the Sierra Nevada as Chinese workers wave a greeting. The Chinese lived and worked in tunnels under the snow, with shafts to give them air and lanterns to light the way. Snowslides occasionally buried camps and crews.

Sierra Nevada. Chinese laborers also played a key role in California's agricultural development. They built hundreds of miles of earthen levees in the Sacramento–San Joaquin River delta patterned after those back home in the Pearl River delta, converting marshes and swamps into productive cropland. And they helped develop the shrimp and abalone industries.

By 1870, there were 63,000 Chinese in the United States, three-quarters of whom lived in California. When the nation's economy collapsed into a severe depression in 1873, the Chinese became scapegoats for the hard times. Chinese competed with unemployed white Americans for jobs and were willing to accept low pay, inflaming anti-Chinese prejudice and resentment. The visible presence of the Chinese—their traditional clothing, even the way they wore their hair—made them convenient targets.

Mobs brandishing clubs, shotguns, and ropes attacked Chinese settlements all over the West, driving people out of their homes, looting, burning, and, at times, shooting or lynching those who refused to leave. During one violent episode, on the night of October 21, 1871, a mob of five hundred white men rampaged through Los Angeles's Chinatown. Although other white men tried to intervene and sympathetic housewives hid their Chinese cooks and servants, by morning, seventeen Chinese had been lynched and two more knifed to death. "The mob was determined to drive [the Chinese] out of the city," the *New York Times* reported.

"Now, what injury have we Chinese done to your honorable people," an immigrant angrily questioned a white friend, "that they should thus turn upon us and make us drink the cup of wrong even to its last poisonous dregs?"

The Chinese fought back. They organized armed militias to defend their communities, formed their own fire brigades, and called general strikes. Chinese vegetable farmers refused to sell their produce, thus depriving white households and hotels of fresh food. Laundrymen returned the laundry neatly folded but still dirty. Chinese leaders appealed to mayors, governors, judges, and newspaper editors for justice and protection. And though they themselves could not testify in court or sit on juries, Chinese filed lawsuits challenging laws designed to harass and oppress them and claiming reparations for their destroyed property.

Politicians, meanwhile, were demanding that Chinese immigrants be excluded from the United States. The Chinese were undesirable aliens, they charged, willing to take on any type of work and to work for longer hours for less pay—depriving whites of jobs. At a California Senate committee hearing in 1876, Chinese immigration was described as an "unarmed invasion" that threatened the entire country. The rallying cry of the Workingmen's Party of California was "The Chinese must go!"

"There were long processions at night," one Chinese immigrant recalled, "with big torch lights and lanterns, carrying the slogan 'The Chinese Must Go,' and mass meetings where fiery tongues flayed the Chinese. . . . We were simply terrified. We kept indoors after dark for fear of being shot in the back."

By 1880, there were more than 100,000 Chinese in the United States. Mounting political pressure resulted in new discriminatory laws aimed at limiting immigration rights for Chinese. In 1882, Congress passed the Chinese Exclusion Act—the first time the United States excluded immigrants because of their nationality or race. Until then, immigration to America had been free and unrestricted for all; newly arrived immigrants had simply walked off the boat and headed for the gold mines. But now,

This political cartoon expresses the anti-Chinese prejudices of the 1880s and the slogan of the Workingmen's Party of California: "The Chinese Must Go." It shows Uncle Sam, holding a proclamation and a can of "magic washer," kicking Chinese out of the United States.

Chinese laborers were no longer allowed to enter the country. The only Chinese exempted from the exclusion law were a select group of diplomats, merchants, students, and teachers, along with members of their families and those claiming to be native-born U.S. citizens.

To enforce the exclusion law, newly appointed immigration officers began to keep detailed records on the movements, occupations, and family relationships of Chinese immigrants. The Geary Act of 1892 required all persons of Chinese descent, including native-born citizens, to carry photo identification cards proving their lawful presence in the United States. At the time, no other group was required to hold such documents.

Chinese community leaders denounced the "Dog Tag Law" and urged Chinese living in the United States to resist it. "The Geary Act is an unjust law," they declared, "and no Chinese should obey it." Risking immediate deportation, Chinese by the thousands refused to register for identity cards in what has been called the largest organized act of civil disobedience in U.S. history. They were supported by white citizens who considered the Geary Act an assault on civil liberties.

When the U.S. Supreme Court ruled that the Geary Act was, in fact, constitutional, community leaders dropped their resistance. They now advised all Chinese residents "to comply with the law"—to register with the government and carry the photo identification cards.

Meanwhile, federal immigration officials screened incoming immigrants for the first time. At San Francisco and other ports of entry, newly arrived Chinese were examined and questioned,

Dressed for a special occasion, a Chinese merchant and his children walk down a street in San Francisco's Chinatown, 1895. Photo by Arnold Genthe.

sometimes for days or even longer. Those who failed to convince the inspectors that they were native-born citizens or members of the exempt classes were refused entry and deported. The Chinese called the exclusion laws the "tyrannical laws." And they complained that immigration officials treated them with suspicion and disrespect.

To protest, merchants in Hong Kong, Shanghai, and other Chinese cities organized a boycott of incoming American goods. The boycott lasted for several months in 1905 and was so effective that the United States finally agreed to relax some of the harsh immigration procedures. President Theodore Roosevelt offered a qualified apology. "In the effort to carry out the policy of excluding Chinese laborers," he said, "grave injustices and wrongs have been done to this nation and to the people of China."

Even so, the Chinese Exclusion Act remained in force, and as the years passed, the act was extended and expanded. When a ship docked in San Francisco, Chinese passengers were taken to a two-story wooden shed at the end of a wharf belonging to the Pacific Mail Steamship Company. There they were held as long as necessary for questioning.

"The Shed—rightly so-called—is a cheap, two-story wooden building at the end of a wharf," a visitor wrote, "built out over the water where the odors of sewage and bilge are most offensive, unclean, at times overrun with vermin, and often inadequate to the number [of immigrants] to be detained."

"Merchants, laborers are all alike penned up, like a flock of sheep . . . for many days, and often weeks," wrote another observer, ". . . and are denied all communication with their own people. . . . A man is imprisoned as a criminal who has committed no crime."

The detention shed had been built to house two hundred detainees, but at times it held as many as five hundred. People fell ill while waiting for their cases to be decided, a few actually died, and some risked their lives to escape. A Chinese-language newspaper in San Francisco reported that one inmate committed suicide "due to the unbearable misery."

Chinese community leaders protested that the detention shed was unsafe and unsanitary. And a protest song lamented that the Chinese alone were being detained:

> *See the Europeans disembark,*
> *Husband's hand on the shoulder of his wife.*
> *See the Japanese disembark*
> *Beaming with pride.*
> *Alas, innocent are we Chinese,*
> *Not allowed to land in America,*
> *Imprisoned, but why?*

One immigration inspector called the detention shed a "fire trap," while another described conditions there as "inhuman." The Commissioner-General of Immigration admitted that the shed was "disgraceful—cramped in dimensions, lacking in every facility for cleanliness and decency." He announced plans to build a new immigration station in San Francisco Bay. It was to be located on Angel Island, a stone's throw from the island occupied by Alcatraz Prison.

Detainees on the steps of the Angel Island hospital.

3

Angel Island or Devil's Island?

For thousands of years, the biggest island in San Francisco Bay was a favorite hunting and fishing ground for the Coast Miwok Indians. Europeans appeared for the first time on a summer morning in 1775, when an expedition led by the Spanish explorer Juan Manuel de Ayala sailed through the Golden Gate and dropped anchor at the island.

Ayala planted a wooden cross and was greeted by a group of Miwoks. Charmed by the hospitality of the Indians, "so constant in their good friendship and so gentle in their manners," and by the "beautiful harmony" of the island's setting and its expansive view of the great bay, Ayala named the place *Isla de los Angeles*—Angel Island.

Under the flag of Spain, then Mexico, and finally the United States, the island became, in succession, a base for whalers and sealers, a cattle ranch, and a U.S. Army camp. In 1910, the Angel Island Immigration Station opened as America's primary immigrant gateway on the Pacific coast.

Angel Island was often called the Ellis Island of the West, but the two immigration stations were very different. Immigrants who passed through Ellis Island in New York Harbor came mainly from Europe. They were usually processed in a few hours or, at most, a few days, and then they boarded a ferry to Manhattan and set out for their new lives.

Immigrants arriving at Angel Island came mainly from China and other parts of Asia. It was the job of inspectors at Angel Island to enforce the strict Chinese exclusion laws, along with other laws passed later that limited immigration from all Asian countries. As a result, Angel Island served as a detention center, where newly arrived immigrants might be held for weeks or months while they tried to prove their legal right to enter the country. "Would it be possible," a Filipino immigrant asked, "for an immigrant like me to become part of the American dream?"

Altogether, over half a million people from more than eighty different countries were processed at Angel Island between 1910 and 1940, when the immigration station closed. Among them were a Mexican woman who gave birth to twins in the Angel Island hospital while waiting to have her papers processed and a Chinese man who hanged himself in a lavatory when he learned that his application for entry would be denied and he would be deported back to China.

When the immigration station opened, the *San Francisco Chronicle* called it "the cleanest, best arranged and in all respects the finest and healthiest emigrant [*sic*] station ever established."

In a full-page article praising the new facility, the *Chronicle* predicted, "Newcomers from foreign shores will probably think they have struck Paradise when they emerge from the steerage quarters of an ocean liner and land at the summer resort which the Immigration Bureau has provided for them."

But not all newcomers regarded the island as a paradise. Immigrants who passed the entry test were free to board the ferry to San Francisco and pursue their vision of the American dream. Others, detained behind fences and barred windows while waiting to learn their fate, had no idea of when, if ever, they would be permitted to enter the United States. They expressed their fears and anguish in poems brushed or carved on the wooden walls.

> *It's been seven weeks since my imprisonment*
> *On this island—and still I do not know when I can land.*
> *Due to the twists and turns of fate,*
> *I have to endure bitterness and sorrow.*

Unlike the Chinese, Korean detainees left no poems on the detention center's walls. But they did publish essays and poems in the newspaper *Sinhan Minbo* (New Korea). The following lines, written under the pen name Cloud, are from a Korean poem titled "Angel Island."

> *Angel Island, Angel Island, all the people said.*
> *So I thought it would be like heaven.*
> *Yet when the iron gate locks with a clang—*
> *It feels like hell.*

Chinese immigrants crowd the deck of a ship as it arrives in San Francisco.

Waves as Big as Mountains

Growing up in southern China, Jann Mon Fong dreamed of seeking his fortune in America. "Every time a big steamer tooted into the harbor," he recalled, "carrying back fellow villagers with their loaded suitcases, we couldn't help but watch with envy the wealth they brought back, the power that could be wielded with money, and the dreams that were realized with it. I, for one, was impressed by their stories of life in the Gold Mountain, which kindled in me the desire to go overseas at a young age."

Most Chinese immigrants at the time were young men who could find jobs in America, work hard, and send money home. Many of them had left wives and children in China. They spent much of their lives overseas, with occasional visits back to their home village. Even a low-paid laundry worker or farm laborer could earn enough in America to support his family in China.

This 1876 illustration from *Harper's Weekly* depicts Chinese immigrants in the steerage compartment of the steamship *Alaska*, bound for San Francisco.

"They told me that anyone who comes to *Gam Saan* will make money fast and go home a rich man," one immigrant explained. "Anyone who comes to America is well respected in China. My family pushed me to come. They wanted me to make a better living."

At first, few Chinese women came to the United States. Both Chinese tradition and the U.S. exclusion laws discouraged female

immigration. Women stayed at home, as custom decreed, raising the children and running the household. But in time, as the restrictions eased and customs changed, more women began to immigrate as the wives and daughters of Chinese merchants and native-born U.S. citizens.

"When my great-grandfather sent for his wife, that was a big, big leap," said Connie Yung Yu, the descendant of a railroad worker. "Women did not leave the village, and she did. And I think . . . my great-grandfather felt there was a future in America and it was a place to have children."

Setting out from their home villages, most immigrants traveled by foot, boat, and train to the busy port of Hong Kong. Few of them could afford a first-class or second-class steamship ticket. They traveled instead in steerage, the dark, cramped, noisy section belowdecks that offered the cheapest accommodations. "We were packed into the ship in one big room," a passenger recalled. "There was no privacy, no comforts, no nothing. We were like silkworms on a tray, eating and sleeping."

The voyage took about three weeks. Often the seas were rough, with "waves as big as mountains." Some passengers were seasick the entire time. They lingered in their bunks, ate little, and had to wash themselves with seawater.

> *For more than twenty days I fed on wind and tasted*
> *waves.*
> *With luck, I arrived safely in the United States.*
> *I thought I could land in a few days.*

*How was I to know that I would become a prisoner
suffering in this wooden building?*

When a ship steamed through the Golden Gate and docked at a San Francisco pier, immigration officials went aboard and inspected the passengers' documents. Those who could show that

A U.S. immigration inspector examines an immigrant's baggage, ca. 1925.

European and Asian immigrants leave the ferry as they arrive at Angel Island, ca. 1925.

they were returning U.S. residents were allowed to collect their baggage and go ashore. The newcomers were transferred to a ferry that carried them across the bay to Angel Island, where they would await hearings on their applications to be landed—that is, to enter the United States.

Filing into the detention center, they were issued identification numbers and assigned to groups. Whites were placed in a separate group. Chinese were segregated from Japanese and other Asians. Men and women, including husbands and wives, were also separated and were not allowed to communicate until their hearings had been concluded. Children under twelve stayed with their mothers. Most of the Chinese immigrants were young men in their teens or twenties. After being escorted to their segregated dormitories, the new arrivals found bunks and settled down to wait for their medical exams and interrogations.

Jann Mon Fong, the boy who dreamed of sailing to America, had his chance to make the voyage in 1931, when he was eighteen. "Braving the winds and waves for twenty days," he wrote to his classmates in China, "the ship finally entered the harbor. Old timers were allowed to land after the immigration inspection. We newcomers had to board another small boat that took us to the detention barracks on Angel Island. We were totally deprived of freedom as soon as we entered the boat. Indeed, those blue-eyed Yankees treated us like pigs and goats!

"My cloth sack on my back and suitcase in my hand, I entered the detention barracks with tears soaking my eyes and cheeks. Resistance? It would not work. First, this was their land, and secondly, I couldn't even speak their language. Immediately, they locked us up in a small room barricaded with barbed wire."

Jann noticed right away that the walls were covered with poems "wherever the hand could reach, even in the toilets and out on the porch where the wood was softer." Fascinated by the poems, by the testimony of those who, like him, had been detained, he copied ninety-nine of them into his notebook during his two-month detention. Another Chinese immigrant, Tet Yee, who spent six months at Angel Island, copied down ninety-six poems.

"The people who wrote the poems did not know what would become of them on Angel Island," Tet Yee explained, "or if they would ever get off the island and make it to San Francisco. The poems were their only means of expressing their inner feelings."

Four days before the Festival of Reunion,
I embarked on the steamship for America.
Time was like an arrow shooting through a cool autumn.
Counting on my fingers, several months have passed,
  leaving me still at the beginning of the road.
I have yet to be interrogated.
My heart is anxious, and weary.

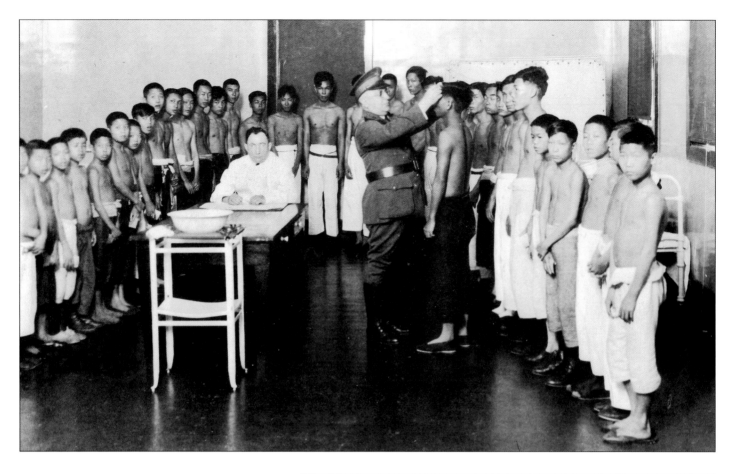

The physical exam: Doctors inspected each immigrant's eyes, ears, nose, and teeth, and conducted stethoscope exams of his or her chest. The clothes that had been worn on the journey, meanwhile, were sent to be disinfected. Many of the new arrivals were teenage boys.

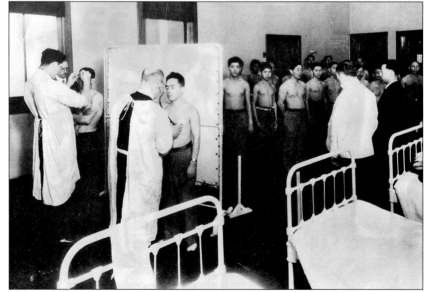

Life in the Detention Barracks

On their first morning at Angel Island, after breakfast, new arrivals were shepherded to the hillside hospital for physical exams. A clean bill of health was necessary before an immigrant could enter the country.

Doctors and nurses inspected each newcomer's ears, nose, and teeth, examined his or her eyes, listened to breathing, searched for signs of contagious disease. If doctors detected an ailment that they could treat effectively, the sick person was admitted to the hospital. Immigrants who were found to have any condition that could not be cured at the time, or that affected their ability to earn a living, were barred from entry and deported.

The hospital had separate facilities for whites and Asians. While European immigrants often breezed through the physical, Asians were subjected to intensive exams on grounds that they were susceptible to parasitic diseases common in rural parts of Asia. The Chinese especially felt that the exams were unnecessarily intrusive. Few Chinese immigrants at the time had experienced Western medicine. It didn't help that the doctors and nurses were dressed in white, the color of funerals in China.

"When we first came, we went to the hospital building for the physical examination," one man remembered. "The doctor told us to take off everything. Really, though, it was humiliating. The Chinese never expose themselves like that. They checked you and checked you. We never got used to that kind of thing—and in front of whites."

Bunks in the detention barracks were stacked three high and could be folded up during the day.

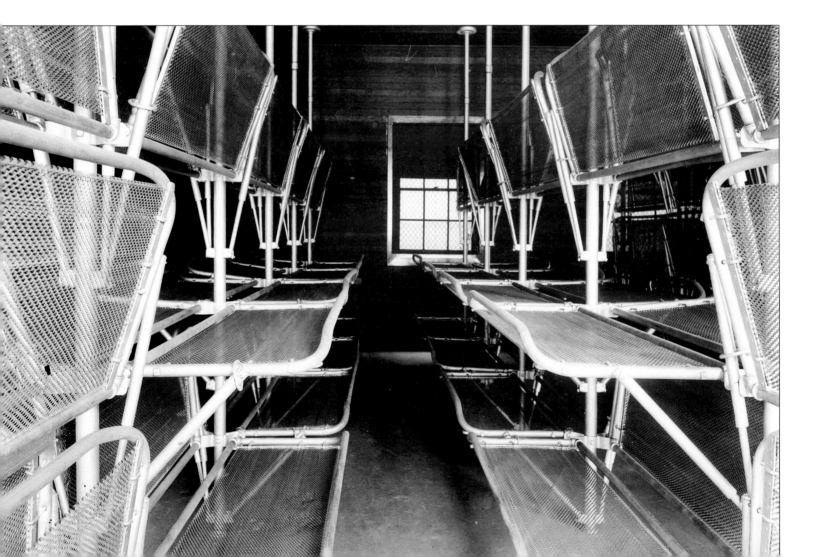

Mealtime in the Asian mess hall.

The jackal doctors checked us for hookworms.
My luck failed; I couldn't go ashore.
Why should a young man regard his life so lightly?
To whom can I plead for redressing such a grave injustice?

Back in their dormitories, those who had passed their physicals settled down to wait for their hearings. They might have to wait two or three weeks before they were called. If their applications for admission were denied and they appealed to the courts, months might pass before their cases were resolved.

"People cried when they saw others who were fortunate enough to leave, especially those of us who had been there a long time," one woman remembered. "I must have cried a bowlful during my stay on Angel Island."

Dormitories were furnished with rows of single bunks, stacked two or three high, that could be folded up during the day. Barred windows looked out onto the bay. The immigrants could see San Francisco to the west and Oakland to the east. Bare lightbulbs hung from the ceilings. One or two Ping-Pong tables stood at one end of each room.

The hallways outside the rooms had tables and chairs where people could chat, play dominoes or chess, or read newspapers and books. Outside the detention barracks were two small fenced-in recreation yards—separate yards for Europeans and for Asians—where detainees could exercise, play volleyball, and enjoy some fresh air.

Longtime detainees had established a Chinese self-governing organization that greeted newcomers, settled disputes, bought phonograph records and mah-jongg sets, and arranged amateur theatricals. "There were presentations of Cantonese opera," a detainee remembered. "We used donated musical instruments. We even had men who would do female impersonations. The open space was also used for sitting or reading. I remember a Mr. Fong, who used to give haircuts for twenty-five cents. He was a barber back home and he had brought all his equipment with him."

As with other facilities, the dining halls were segregated by race. Chinese detainees were served Chinese dishes, but the kitchen wasn't equipped to cook the meals in the traditional manner.

"They just steamed the food until it was like a soupy stew," one woman complained. "After looking at it you'd lose your appetite!"

Detainees often complained about the food, and at least once, a near riot broke out when everyone started throwing dishes

Chinese immigrant children, ca. 1925.

around the dining hall. Troops from nearby Fort McDowell on the island had to be called in to restore order.

But others remembered that the meals were filling and welcome. "Because there had not been enough for us to eat in China," said one man, "I enjoyed the meals at Angel Island."

"Often at meal time we could hear the men, their footsteps, coming up the stairs," one woman remembered. "As they walked up, some would call out to their wives loudly, just once or twice. That was how they kept in touch."

Many of the Chinese were adolescent boys with huge appetites who could hardly wait for the next meal. "Breakfast was served at nine," recalled a detainee who was fifteen at the time. "By 8:30, everyone would gather at the door, fighting to be first. Sometimes, when the guard was a few minutes late opening the door, the bad ones would kick the door and shout, 'Hey, we want to eat! Are you trying to starve us?' . . . As soon as the man opened the door, he would have to stand aside or be knocked over. It was like letting the cattle out. Speaking of it now, I'm embarrassed."

There were some who endured their wait with resignation. "Every person had to be patient," one woman said, "and tell herself, 'I'm just being delayed, it doesn't matter.'" Others would remember Angel Island as a prison, where they could only stare at the sea and sky beyond the barbed wire, dream about their families back home, and worry about how to pay off the money they had borrowed for their trips to America.

> *Day after day, a prisoner in this wooden house,*
> *My freedom in chains—I can't bear to talk about it.*

I look around for a happy face among those who only sit
   in silence.
I am anxious and depressed and cannot fall asleep.
The days are endless, the bottle always empty, my sadness
   unrelieved.
Nights are long, the pillow cold; who can comfort my
   solitude?
Having drunk so deeply from this well of loneliness and
   bitterness,
Shouldn't I just return home and learn to plow the fields?

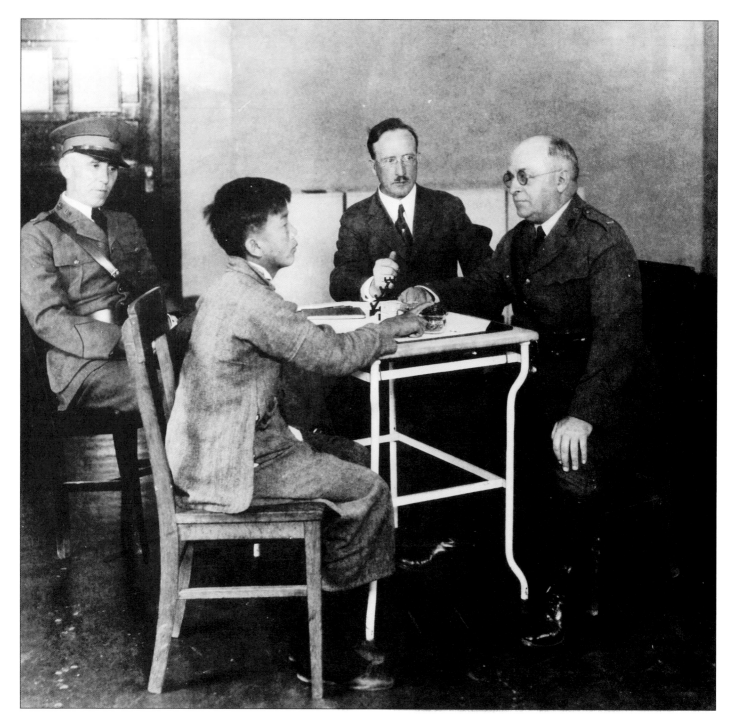

Facing the interrogators: An interrogation could last from less than an hour to several days and might include hundreds of questions.

The Interrogation

"After two weeks, I was called in for interrogation," an immigrant recalled. "I waited a long while downstairs before it was my turn."

When the time came, the detainee was led into a large room and asked to take a seat. Waiting for him were two or three inspectors, who asked questions; an interpreter; and a stenographer, who typed a word-by-word record of the hearing. After the immigrant was sent back to the detention barracks, the inspectors decided whether he or she would be allowed to enter the United States or deported.

Many Chinese found ways to get around the exclusion laws. Some traveled to Canada or Mexico and were then smuggled into the United States. Others obtained false papers showing that they were the foreign-born children of U.S. citizens. They became known as "paper sons."

Coaching notes to help detainees answer interrogators' questions were smuggled onto the island. The notes were picked up from relatives of the detainees in San Francisco and taken back to the island by members of the Chinese kitchen staff. This message is shown with the hollowed-out orange in which it was hidden.

"We didn't want to come in illegally, but we were forced to because of the immigration laws," one man remembered. "They picked on the Chinese. . . . So we had to take the crooked path." For a majority of Chinese immigrants at the time, the "crooked path" was the only way they could gain entry to the United States.

Under the exclusion laws, Chinese could be admitted only as members of the exempt classes, as native-born U.S. citizens, or as the wives or foreign-born children of citizens. Chinese men working in the United States often went back to their home villages to find wives and start families. Those who had been born in America were automatically citizens; even if their children were born in China, they too were citizens eligible to enter the United States.

And yet reliable birth records were scarce. It wasn't easy to determine who was or was not a native-born citizen. Because Chinese women often delivered their babies at home, many Chinese did not have birth certificates. And in 1906, the great San Francisco earthquake and fire destroyed the city's birth records. Chinese men already living in the United States could now claim that they had been born in San Francisco. Citizenship meant that they had the right to bring their families from China to join them. As a result, Chinese who applied for admission as citizens or family members of citizens faced much tougher interrogations than immigrants of other nationalities.

"There is not much way of checking on the Chinese when they get in here," an immigration official reported. "A number will have papers, a number will not have papers, and when asked why, they say they were born in San Francisco."

It was the job of the inspectors to ferret out false claims of citizenship. They questioned the applicant and also, separately, each family member he hoped to join in America, who served as his witnesses. The interrogation could be so difficult that applicants might rehearse for months in China, even when their claim to citizenship was perfectly valid. Those who were paper sons or paper daughters studied special coaching books. They had to learn about the family and village they were pretending to be from. They memorized answers to every conceivable question. And they carried coaching notes aboard the ship during their voyage to America, and threw them overboard before the ship docked.

"My paper father told me that I would be interrogated for sure," recalled Mock Ging Sing. "He said, 'They will ask many, many questions. . . . You better memorize the coaching book well. If you don't, you'll make mistakes. And once you make mistakes, it's all over.'"

The burden of proof was on the immigrant, who had to convince the inspectors that he was the person his papers claimed him to be.

"I was ten years old," recalled Ark Chin, "and to be brought into a room and you see this big Lo Fan [Caucasian]—you know, the devil, so to speak—it was kind of overpowering."

The applicant was questioned about his birth, his parents, his brothers and sisters, his family home, his village. The interrogation might be brief, or it might drag out for three or four days and fill dozens of pages of typewritten testimony. "Usually you would start with the immigrant himself," said one inspector, "and check his testimony against his relatives. If the testimonies matched, we had to give them the benefit of the doubt."

If a son said that his father had two brothers, and the father, questioned separately, said three brothers, then the applicant was in trouble. "There was just one way of finding out if the family belonged together as it was claimed," explained an inspector, "and that was by testing their knowledge of their relationship."

"They even asked me where the rice bin was kept," an immigrant remembered. "Can you imagine? If your father had said the left side and the son, the right side, that wouldn't do."

Chinese women with their babies wait to be interviewed. Sitting with them is Deaconess Katherine Maurer, a Methodist missionary known as "the angel of Angel Island," who ministered to detainees from 1912 to 1940.

Even a correct answer might arouse suspicion, as in this actual exchange:

Immigration officers question a Japanese man as his newly arrived bride waits silently behind him.

Q: Is your house one story or two stories?
A: There is an attic.
Q: Are there steps to the attic?
A: Yes.
Q: How many?
A: Twelve.
Q: How do you know?
A: I counted them, because I was told you would ask me questions like these.
Q: Then you were coached in the answers to be given?

You rehearsed and memorized the information to make us think you are the son of Wong Hing?

A: No, no, no. I was not coached. I am the true son of Wong Hing, my father, who is now in San Francisco. He told me that you would ask questions like these and that I was to be prepared to answer in the most minute detail.

Some applicants were interrogated two or three times. "After each question, the interrogator would stop for a long time and look at my expression before continuing. It took more than an hour for each interrogation."

Others sped through the hearing in a few minutes: "It took not more than ten minutes. They asked a few questions, nothing

Immigrants released from detention board the government ferry at Angel Island, heading for the mainland after passing inspection.

much. . . . Maybe they asked less questions than usual because they had questioned my husband first."

When the interrogations ended, the applicant went back to the detention barracks to await the verdict. If a guard came in, called out a person's name, and shouted in Chinese "Good fortune!" or "Go ashore!," it meant that the immigrant had passed and was free to enter the country. But if a person was to be deported, the guard would call his name, then silently make motions as if he were crying.

According to one inspector, more than 75 percent of Chinese applicants passed their Angel Island interrogation. Those who were rejected could appeal to the courts or to higher immigration authorities in Washington, D.C., and most appeals were successful. "Probably only 5 percent of those denied were ever really deported," the inspector said. "Some who were deported came back and tried again and made it."

For those who weren't admitted, deportation was a personal calamity. Some rejects wrote despairing poems on the walls as they awaited their fate, and a few tried to take their own lives. A witness to a suicide in the men's barracks reported: "The guy who hung himself knew he was going to be deported after questioning and if he had gone back to China he would have been seen as a failure."

> *Oh, poor me. Barred from landing,*
> *fearful of being deported back to China.*
> *There is no way for me to face the elders east of the river.*
> *I anticipated wealth, but it's only poverty, alas, that I've*
> *reaped.*

Japanese picture brides, ca. 1925. More than ten thousand Japanese
women sailed to America to live with husbands they had never met.
The unidentified man in the photograph may be a representative
from the Japanese consulate in San Francisco.

7

Picture Brides, Freedom Fighters, and Refugees

Writing in his diary, a Japanese immigrant took note of the many languages he heard spoken in the Angel Island detention barracks:

> [I] *hear sounds of different voices from the next rooms*
> *Chinese, Russian, Mexican, Greek, and Italian*
> *Voices of sorrow, nostalgia, rage, and passion.*

After the Chinese, the Japanese were the second-largest group to pass through Angel Island. They came at first as farmers and laborers escaping hard times back home. Like the Chinese before them, they were accused of stealing jobs from white workers and competing unfairly with white farmers. By the 1920s, Japanese were subject to new discriminatory laws that restricted immigration not only from China and Japan but also from a vast geographical region called the Asiatic Barred Zone, which stretched from India across Asia to the Polynesian Islands.

Japanese already living in the United States were allowed to send for family members. Thousands of unmarried Japanese men took advantage of this rule through the custom of arranged marriages—in this case, long-distance arranged marriages. Rather than travel back to Japan to look for a bride, a man relied on relatives to find a suitable match for him. After an exchange of photos and a wedding ceremony in which the bride's name was entered into the groom's family register, the marriage was considered legal in Japan. When these "picture brides" first arrived in the United States, they had to be remarried according to U.S. laws, a requirement that was later dropped.

Thousands of young Japanese women sailed to America to live with husbands they had never met. Arriving in San Francisco, dressed for the occasion in their finest kimonos, they were greeted by eager husbands holding photographs and craning their necks as they searched for their brides, while the brides in turn tried to match the photos they were holding to a face in the crowd of men waiting anxiously on the dock.

"My husband was sixteen years older than I," one woman recalled. "I did not think about whether he would be a good husband or not. In Japan it was the custom to arrange marriages. This being so, there was no alternative."

Before the brides could be released to their husbands, they were ferried to Angel Island for their physical exams and interrogations. In most cases, they were admitted to the United States

Deaconess Katherine Maurer conducts an English-language class for a group of female immigrants, 1933.

within a day or so. Even so, for many of these young women who had led sheltered lives with their families in Japan, it was an unsettling experience. "I had never seen such a prison-like place," said one. "We all cried and cried," another remembered, "because we didn't know when we'd be free and because we couldn't understand anything they said to us."

Picture brides from China and Korea also came to America. Like the Japanese, they sometimes discovered that their intended husbands, waiting anxiously on the dock in their best suits, were much older than their photos had suggested.

"When I first saw my fiancé, I could not believe my eyes," said Anna Choi, who was fifteen when she became a picture bride.

"His hair was grey, and I could not see any resemblance to the picture I had. He was a lot older than I had imagined . . . but I did not have it in my heart to disappoint or hurt such a middle-aged man like him . . . he was forty-six years old."

According to eyewitnesses, some brides fainted when they saw their bridegrooms; some wept, crying "Oh dear me, what shall I do?"; and some refused to land and returned home.

Given time, most picture brides adjusted to their new lives, so far from the familiar comforts of the families they had left behind. A young Japanese bride, just arrived in California's San Joaquin Valley, remembered standing alone in the darkness outside her house: "If I looked really hard I could see, faintly glowing in the distance, one tiny light. And over there, I could see another. And over there another. And I knew that that was where people lived. More than feeling *sabishii* [lonely], I felt *samui* [cold]. It was so lonely it was beyond loneliness. It was cold."

✺ ✺ ✺

Young political activists who today would be called freedom fighters also came to the United States by way of Angel Island. Some were South Asians working to free India from British colonial rule. Most of them entered the country as students, joined the Gadar ("revolutionary") party, and traveled widely, visiting South Asian communities on the Pacific Coast and urging their countrymen to support the cause of India's independence.

U.S. immigration officials, under pressure from the British government, kept a close eye on the revolutionary Gadar movement.

Southeast Asian immigrants—men, women, and one child—wearing traditional clothing, on the steps of the Angel Island administration building.

Shortly before the United States entered World War I in 1917, several leaders of the movement were arrested in San Francisco, prosecuted, and imprisoned for conspiracy to violate America's neutrality laws. Supporters of Indian independence had to wait until after World War II to achieve their goal.

Korean activists, meanwhile, were working to overthrow Japanese colonial rule in their homeland. One Korean couple, members of a secret patriotic society, narrowly escaped capture and torture by the Japanese police. They disguised themselves as Russian refugees, crossed the frozen Yalu River in the dead of winter, and took a train to Shanghai, where they boarded a ship bound for San Francisco. On board they dressed in Chinese clothes and pretended to be Chinese immigrants. The ship made three stops in Japan, but they managed to pass undetected when Japanese police came on board to rout out any Koreans.

"When I left Korea, I felt like a free man," Whang Sa Sung told his granddaughter sixty years later. "Korea was like a jail, and I was a prisoner. I wanted to come to America. America was a free country."

When Korea won independence in 1945, Whang, living in San Francisco, was honored for his service to the Korean independence movement. He refused to accept the honor, saying, "I have not done enough . . . there were many patriots who gave their lives during the Japanese occupation and they are the ones to be honored. . . . The struggle for independence has been every Korean's duty and I have done merely that."

During World War I, refugees fleeing from the chaos of the 1917 Russian Revolution made their way across Siberia to the Chinese cities of Harbin and Shanghai and from there to Japan, where they boarded ships bound for San Francisco. Many of them arrived with little or no money. They were detained at Angel Island until they could convince immigration inspectors that they would not become public charges, unable to support themselves, and were not secret agents of a revolutionary organization.

Russian immigrant women with their children.

No one escaped scrutiny, not even the famous composer Sergei Prokofiev, who left Russia early in 1918. He spent four months traveling across Siberia by train, then waiting for visas for Japan and the United States, then trying to book passage for San Francisco. By the time he arrived in foggy San Francisco Bay, the Russian currency, the ruble, had lost half its value, and he had barely enough money left to continue on to New York. And he was in "a bad temper," as he put it, when he stepped off the ship and was ferried to Angel Island along with other Russian arrivals.

His mood only got worse when he was assigned to a room with barred windows. "Although the door was delicately left half-open," he wrote later, "the impression was nevertheless unpleasant." Prokofiev was detained two nights while waiting to be interrogated. When his turn came, he was asked, among other questions: "Are you a member of any organization?"

"Yes," he replied, "the Petrograd [now St. Petersburg] Chess Society."

"Are you a member of a political party?"

When he replied that he was not, he was asked, "Why?"

"Because I consider that an artist should be outside politics."

"Have you ever been in jail?"

"Yes. In yours."

Despite his grumpiness, Prokofiev was admitted to the United States. And he never forgot his "unpleasant" entry into America or his "exile" at Angel Island.

A generation later, as World War II approached, Angel Island became, by way of China, a gateway to America for hundreds of Jewish refugees fleeing persecution in Nazi Germany. They first escaped to Shanghai, one of the few places that would admit Jewish refugees. There they waited for months or years to receive visas that would allow them to enter the United States. The fortunate ones made it to America before the U.S. State Department, fearing the infiltration of Nazi spies into the country, stopped issuing visas to refugees in July 1941.

Those who landed safely in America entered a new life through Angel Island. "I was lucky all the way," remembered Alice Steiner, who reached the welcoming pier of Angel Island in 1940, shortly before the immigration station closed. "A great part of my family who were older died in the Holocaust."

Alice settled with her family in the San Francisco Bay area, because, she always explained, she thought of the bay and Angel Island as the most beautiful spot on earth.

On August 12, 1940, the Angel Island administration building burned to the ground, destroying all of its records. Soon afterward, the immigration station closed for good.

A Nation of Immigrants

At midnight on August 12, 1940, an electrical fire broke out in the basement of the Angel Island administration building. The building was destroyed, although firemen were able to save the adjoining detention barracks and the hospital. Rather than rebuild, the government chose to close the immigration station and move its services to a new facility in San Francisco.

For years afterward, the barracks and hospital stood empty and abandoned, embraced by morning fogs and decorated with graffiti by passing hikers. Eventually, Angel Island became a California state park. The remains of the administration building were cleared away, and the immigration station's surviving buildings were scheduled for demolition.

Meanwhile, the nation's immigration laws were changing. During World War II, China became an ally of the United States, and in 1943, as a gesture of friendship,

Congress repealed the Chinese exclusion laws. For the first time, Chinese immigrants could apply to become naturalized citizens. "China is our ally," President Franklin D. Roosevelt declared. "By the repeal of the Chinese exclusion laws, we can correct a historic mistake."

Other changes in the laws followed, resulting in the 1965 Immigration Act, passed in an era of civil rights activism. This act abolished racial discrimination in American immigration law, putting Chinese and all other Asians on an equal footing with immigrants from Europe and Latin America.

And then, in 1970, California park ranger Alexander Weiss happened upon the decaying walls of poetry in the dark, littered, and abandoned detention building. He alerted friends in the Asian American community to visit the wall poems and photograph them before the building was torn down. They recognized the historical significance of the site instantly and launched a campaign to rescue the Angel Island Immigration Station from the wrecker's ball.

"We needed to save the immigration station to remind us of the tough times some immigrants had in coming to this country," Weiss said. "They were treated shabbily, but they actually made this country a better place. That's why we need memorials . . . so that we will learn from our past."

Members of the Asian American community formed the Angel Island Immigration Station Historical Advisory Committee. They lobbied the California legislature for funds to restore the site and recruited volunteers to contribute their skills to the restoration project. Architects and historians collaborated on preservation

San Diego History Center

Chinese Cong. Mission
San Diego Calif. 2-21-26.

Three generations of Chinese Americans at the Congregational
Chinese Mission, San Diego, California, February 21, 1926.

plans. Scholars collected and translated into English the poems carved into the walls. Angel Island descendants interviewed former detainees and officials who had worked at the station.

"This is our Plymouth Rock," the advisory committee declared, "our Valley Forge, our Alamo, our Statue of Liberty, our Lincoln Memorial, all rolled into one."

In 1997, as the reclamation efforts moved forward, the federal government recognized Angel Island as a National Historic Landmark. Finally, on February 15, 2009 — nearly forty years after Weiss first saw the wall poems — the newly restored site was opened to the public.

"The immigration station is a site of conscience, about immigration past, present, and future," said Kathy Lim Ko, president of the Angel Island Immigration Station Foundation. "It is . . . a place of reconciliation for the wrongs that were done and the human rights that we must uphold."

Three years after the opening, the U.S. House of Representatives issued a rare apology. On June 18, 2012 — 130 years after the passage of the Chinese Exclusion Act — the House expressed its regret for enacting discriminatory laws targeting Chinese immigrants. California representative Judy Chu, the first Chinese American woman elected to Congress, sponsored the resolution.

"It is for my grandfather and for all Chinese Americans who were told for six decades by the U.S. government that the land of the free wasn't open to them that we must pass this resolution," she told her fellow lawmakers. "We must finally and formally acknowledge these ugly laws that were incompatible with

America's founding principles. By doing so, we will acknowledge that discrimination has no place in our society."

To call attention to the resolution, Chu held a press conference in downtown Los Angeles, at the site of the 1871 Chinese Massacre, in which nineteen Chinese immigrants lost their lives.

Today, the reclaimed Angel Island Immigration Station welcomes all visitors. The old detention barracks are now a museum where the wall poems have been lovingly preserved. While the building houses uncomfortable memories, it pays tribute to the courage and perseverance of those who once were detained there, reminding us that the United States is, and always has been, a nation of immigrants who adopt this land as their new home.

> *I raise my brush and write a poem to tell my wife,*
> *In the middle of last night, I sighed at our being apart.*
> *The affectionate murmuring of your concern remains with*
>   *me.*
> *I have no idea if ever I'll return home in triumph.*

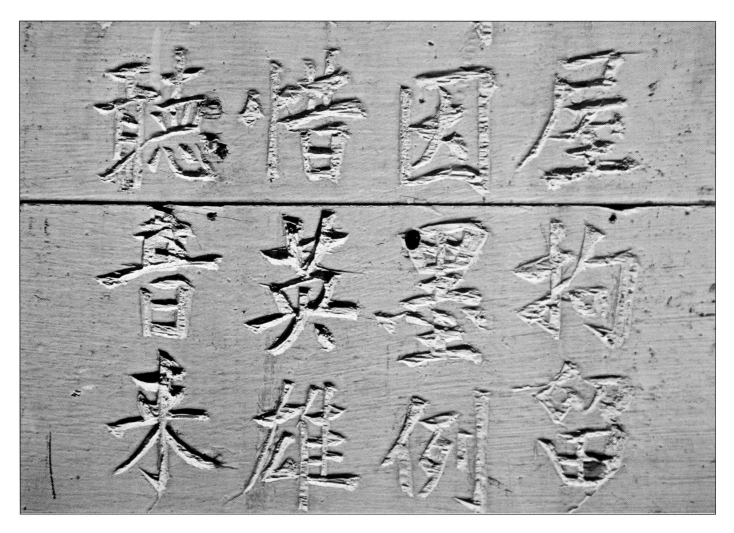

Close-up of a wall carving in the detention barracks.

9

Visiting Angel Island

A visitor today arrives at Angel Island in the same manner as the immigrants of yesterday—by boat. Regularly scheduled ferries leave from Pier 41 in San Francisco and from the town of Tiburon in Marin County. Passengers disembark at Ayala Cove. From there they can hike to the immigration station, a mile and a half away along a road that offers sweeping views of the bay. A shuttle service from the Ayala Café is available in season.

Volunteer docents offer guided tours of the Detention Barracks Museum. Visitors can examine the men's and women's dormitories, where so many human dramas unfolded. Carefully preserved and illuminated poems are etched into every wall. The original floor-to-ceiling metal poles to which bunks stacked three high were attached still stand. Reproductions of typical bunks are made up with blankets and pillows, while suitcases, articles of clothing, family photographs, playing cards, gaming tiles, and keepsakes are piled under the bunks and scattered about the room. Large interpretive panels discuss the challenges the immigrants faced and the important role of poetry in Chinese social history.

The visitors' center at Ayala Cove offers maps, brochures, books, and photographs. Two twenty-minute films are screened in the viewing room—one covers the history and natural beauty of the island; the other, *Carved in Silence*, tells the story of the wall poems and the island's role in American immigration history.

For information concerning museum hours, admission fees, and group tours, see www.aiisf.org/visit.

Ferry service from San Francisco: www.blueandgoldfleet.com.

Ferry service from Tiburon: www.angelislandferry.com.

An immigrant boy at Angel Island.

從今遠

各江瑜君無歡歡
苦遠其西

報殺辛勤變如麗

Source Notes

The following notes refer to the sources of quoted material. Each citation includes the first and last words or phrases of the quotation and the source. Unless otherwise noted, all references are to works cited in the Selected Bibliography. Quotations from Lowe and Moyers are from verbal interviews in those video documentaries. Wall poems have been translated from the Chinese ideograms as transcribed in *Island*.

Abbreviations used:

Angel Island: Erika Lee and Judy Yung, *Angel Island*
Barde: Robert Eric Barde, *Immigration at the Golden Gate*
Chang: Iris Chang, *The Chinese in America*
Choy: Bong-youn Choy, *Koreans in America*
Eldredge: Zoeth S. Eldredge and E. J. Molera, *The March of Portola*

Gates: Erika Lee, *At America's Gates*

Island: Him Mark Lai et al., *Island*

Larson: Jane Leung Larson, "The United States as a Site for Baohuanghui Activism"

Lowe: Felicia Lowe, *Carved in Silence*

Moyers: Bill Moyers, *Becoming American*

Pfaelzer: Jean Pfaelzer, *Driven Out*

Press: Stephen Press, "Prokofiev's Vexing Entry into the USA"

Takaki: Ronald Takaki, *Strangers from a Different Shore*

Yen: Ching-hwang Yen, *Coolies and Mandarins*

1. WHERE THE WALLS SPEAK

page

2 "I looked around . . . all over": *Angel Island*, p. 302

3 "a bunch of graffiti": *Angel Island*, p. 302

5 "Actually . . . [help save them]": *Angel Island*, p. 303

"They were all . . . talk about it": *Angel Island*, p. 303

"I really felt . . . to be saved": *Angel Island*, p. 304

2. BOUND FOR GOLD MOUNTAIN

7–8 "There were four . . . the rice": Takaki, p. 33

8 "Our baggage . . . possessions": Moyers, Program 1: *Gold Mountain Dreams*

"California for Americans!": Takaki, p. 81

"washed-out": Pfaelzer, p. 45

11–12 "The mob . . . the city": Pfaelzer, p. 53

"Now, what injury . . . dregs?": Takaki, p. 112

"unarmed invasion": *Gates*, p. 23

12 "The Chinese must go!": Pfaelzer, p. 78

"There were long . . . the back": Moyers, Program 1: *Gold Mountain Dreams*

14 "Dog Tag Law": Pfaelzer, p. 291

"The Geary Act . . . obey it": Pfaelzer, p. 291

"to comply with the law": Pfaelzer, p. 329

16 "tyrannical laws": *Island*, p. 12

"In the effort . . . of China": *Gates*, p. 126

"The Shed . . . detained": Barde, p. 68

16–17 "Merchants, laborers . . . no crime": Yen, p. 304

17 "due to . . . misery": Barde, p. 74

"See the Europeans . . . Imprisoned, but why?": Larson; translation by Renquin Yu from UCLA Digital online document: digital2.library.ucla.edu/viewItem .do?ark=21198/zz00253t3n

"fire trap" and "inhuman": *Angel Island*, p. 11

"disgraceful . . . decency": Barde, p. 68

3. ANGEL ISLAND OR DEVIL'S ISLAND?

19 "so constant . . . beautiful harmony": Eldredge, quoted from *The Log of the San Carlos*

20 "Would it be . . . American dream?": Takaki, p. 18

20–21 "the cleanest . . . for them": Barde, p. 15

21 *"It's been seven . . . sorrow"*: Anonymous, "Poem Number 17," *Island*, p. 154

"Angel Island . . . feels like hell": *Angel Island*, p. 199, translated by Jikyung Hwang and Charles Egan

4. WAVES AS BIG AS MOUNTAINS

23 "Every time . . . young age": *Angel Island*, p. 72

24 "They told me . . . better living": *Angel Island*, p. 71

25 "When my great-grandfather . . . have children": Moyers, Program 1: *Gold Mountain Dreams*

"We were packed . . . sleeping": Takaki, p. 70

"waves as big as mountains": *Island*, p. 42

25–26 *"For more . . . wooden building"*: Anonymous, "Poem Number 7," *Island*, p. 38

28 "Braving the winds . . . barbed wire": *Angel Island*, p. 76

"wherever the hand . . . softer": *Angel Island*, p. 103

29 "The people . . . feelings": *Angel Island*, p. 103

"Four days . . . and weary": *Island*, p. 36

5. LIFE IN THE DETENTION BARRACKS

32 "When we first . . . whites": *Angel Island*, p. 39

33 *"The jackal doctors . . . injustice"*: Anonymous, "Poem Number 51," *Island*, p. 164

33–34 "People cried . . . Angel Island": *Island*, p. 72

34 "There were presentations . . . with him": *Island*, p. 74

35 "They just steamed . . . appetite!": *Island*, p. 79

36 "Because there had not . . . Angel Island": *Island*, p. 79

"Often at meal time . . . kept in touch": Lowe, *Carved in Silence*

"Breakfast was served . . . embarrassed": *Island*, p. 79

"Every person . . . doesn't matter'": *Island*, p. 74

36–37 *"Day after day . . . the fields"*: Anonymous, "Poem Number 32," *Island*, p. 68

6. THE INTERROGATION

39 "After two weeks . . . my turn": *Island*, p. 118

"paper sons": *Gates*, p. 4

40 "We didn't want . . . crooked path": *Angel Island*, p. 84

"There is not . . . San Francisco": *Gates*, p. 102

41 "My paper father . . . it's all over": Lowe, *Carved in Silence*

"I was ten . . . overpowering": Moyers, Program 2: *Between Two Worlds*

"Usually you would . . . doubt": *Island*, p. 11

42 "There was just . . . relationship": *Island*, p. 113

"They even asked . . . that wouldn't do": *Island*, p. 116

43–44 "Is your house . . . minute detail": Chang, p. 150

44 "After each question . . . interrogation": *Island*, p. 117

44–45 "It took . . . husband first": *Island*, p. 118

45 "Good fortune!" and "Go ashore!": *Island*, p. 109

"Probably only . . . made it": *Island*, p. 111

"The guy . . . failure": *Angel Island*, p. 101

"Oh, poor me . . . reaped": Anonymous, "Poem Number 61," *Island*, p. 126

7. PICTURE BRIDES, FREEDOM FIGHTERS, AND REFUGEES

47 *"[I] hear . . . passion"*: *Angel Island*, p. 112

48 "picture brides": Takaki, p. 72

"My husband . . . alternative": *Angel Island*, p. 118

49 "I had never . . . said to us": *Angel Island*, p. 120

49–50 "When I first saw . . . forty-six years old": Choy, p. 321

50 "Oh dear me . . . do?": Choy, p. 89

"If I looked . . . It was cold": Takaki, pp. 73–74

52 "When I left . . . free country": Takaki, p. 54

"I have not . . . merely that": Choy, pp. 302–3

54 "a bad temper . . . unpleasant . . . exile": Press

55 "I was lucky . . . Holocaust": *Angel Island*, p. 244

8.   A NATION OF IMMIGRANTS

58 "China . . . historic mistake": Takaki, p. 377

"We needed . . . our past": *Angel Island*, pp. 303–4

60 "This is our . . . into one": *Angel Island*, p. 307

"The immigration station . . . must uphold": *Angel Island*, p. 313

60–61 "It is for . . . our society": *Los Angeles Times*, June 18, 2012

61 *"I raise . . . triumph"*: Anonymous, "Poem Number 26," *Island*, p. 156

Selected Bibliography

PUBLISHED SOURCES

Barde, Robert Eric. *Immigration at the Golden Gate: Passenger Ships, Exclusion, and Angel Island*. Westport, Conn.: Praeger, 2008.

Chang, Iris. *The Chinese in America: A Narrative History*. New York: Viking, 2003.

Choy, Bong-youn. *Koreans in America*. Chicago: Nelson-Hall, 1979.

Eldredge, Zoeth S., and E. J. Molera. *The March of Portola and the Discovery of the Bay of San Francisco*. San Francisco: California Promotion Committee, 1909.

Lai, Him Mark, Genny Lim, and Judy Yung. *Island: Poetry and History of Chinese Immigrants on Angel Island, 1910–1940*. Seattle: University of Washington Press, 1991.

Lee, Erika. *At America's Gates: Chinese Immigration During the Exclusion Era, 1882–1943*. Chapel Hill: University of North Carolina Press, 2003.

Lee, Erika, and Judy Yung. *Angel Island: Immigrant Gateway to America*. New York: Oxford University Press, 2010.

Pfaelzer, Jean. *Driven Out: The Forgotten War Against Chinese Americans*. Berkeley: University of California Press, 2008.

Press, Stephen. "Prokofiev's Vexing Entry into the USA." *Three Oranges Journal* 6 (November 2003): www.sprkfv.net /journal/three06/vexing1.html.

Takaki, Ronald. *Strangers from a Different Shore: A History of Asian Americans*, rev. ed. Boston: Little, Brown, 1998.

Yen, Ching-hwang. *Coolies and Mandarins: China's Protection of Overseas Chinese During the Late Ch'ing Period (1851– 1911)*. Singapore: Singapore University Press, 1985.

Yep, Laurence, and Kathleen S. Yep. *The Dragon's Child: A Story of Angel Island*. New York: HarperCollins, 2008.

VIDEO RECORDINGS

Felicia Lowe, producer-director. *Carved in Silence*. San Francisco: Lowedown Productions, 1987. DVD, 45 min.

A Bill Moyers Special, *Becoming American: The Chinese Experience*. Princeton, N.J.: Films for the Humanities and Sciences, 2003. 3 DVDs, 360 min.

UNPUBLISHED

Larson, Jane Leung. "The United States as a Site for Baohuanghui Activism." Paper presented at the Fifth Annual Conference of Institutes and Libraries in Chinese Overseas Studies, World Confederation of Institutes and Libraries in Chinese Overseas Studies, Vancouver, British Columbia, May 17, 2012.

Acknowledgments

Some years ago, California librarian Milly Lee suggested that I write a book about the Angel Island Immigration Station. She referred me to people who were active in the campaign to preserve the site's buildings and history and sent me books and news clippings that I might find useful. "You should never ask a librarian what she knows about a subject," she wrote. "She'll pester you forever with more—more—more!"

Other projects intervened, and for a time the subject remained on the shelf. Meanwhile, the campaign to preserve Angel Island as a National Historic Landmark succeeded, the newly restored site was opened to the public, and books, articles, and research materials continued to appear. So I figured the time had come. I am grateful to Milly Lee for calling my attention to this once-neglected subject with a persistence and enthusiasm that gave me the confidence to undertake this book.

I am indebted also to the volunteers who worked to save,

photograph, and record the wall poems in the detention barracks, and to Evans Chan, who translated especially for this book some poems from the Chinese transcriptions printed in *Island*. Interviews with former detainees and employees of the immigration station, some of which are cited here, were conducted and translated from the Cantonese by Him Mark Lai, Genny Lim, and Judy Yung, co-editors of *Island*, initially published in 1980 by the HOC DOI (History of Chinese Detained On Island) project, and the seminal work on the history of the Angel Island Immigration Station.

My thanks also to Meng Tam for her insights on Chinese American immigration, and to Wil Jorae, museum curator at the California State Parks Photographic Archives, for help in obtaining many of the photos included here.

Picture Credits

末屋於雷

新以壼鈉

可譜英雄無開武

以慈音本笑病轗

Index

Page numbers in *italics* refer to photos and illustrations.